Introduction

This book aims to help reduce the fear, guilt and isolation o
late stage dementia and end of life.

It provides practical ways to encourage you to be there, saying and doing the
right things, right up until the end; fulfilling wishes and desires to ensure the
person you are caring for receives the best quality of care and attention they
require and deserve.

The activities will enable everyone to communicate in a non-verbal way which in
turn will be rewarding for families, providing them with a sense of closure,
reducing the stress and fear often associated with end of life.

Allow the experience to be uplifting, not depressing or too overwhelming and
use only things that will bring comfort and peace as the days slip gracefully away.

Please be there....

1 3 1678139 0

This may comfort you in your time of loss....

Mum's Angel Poem

An angel descended from heaven one day
and decided to take my mummy away

He folded his wings around her in strife
and stole from my heart a piece of my life

The wings that wrapped round her and took her away
leave feathers for collection each lonely day

They help me to face all the sadness inside and know
that an angel is there as my guide

Her presence is felt in many a day
as her hands touch my face in a cobweb – like way

She follows me round in work and in play
and I chat and ask guidance as to what I should say

I look in the mirror and what do I see,
my mother is standing there staring at me

The clarity of skin and depth of her eyes
is this really my mother in certain disguise

She carried me with her and gave life to me
and protected me always and now I can see

That she'll always be with me whenever I'm low
and show me she loves me in the way that I know

A feather her token she leaves unto me,
an aura or sighting I may sometimes not see

The darkest of corners she lights in my room,
her tenderness likens the place to a womb

No shivers are with me when I feel she is near,
her tender touch strokes me and brings me no fear

An angel she is in this world full of hate,
she's always around me and I cannot wait

To meet once more with her in her heavenly place
when one day I'm chosen, those wings will embrace

So please don't stop visiting me here on this plane,
your closeness and presence help lessen the pain

Fiona Mahoney (2004)

Please don't forget about me from now until the day I am no longer by your side

I do not want to feel lonely or sad without someone to comfort me even if I do not initiate it or respond

Smile and laugh at me

Celebrate anniversaries, special days, birthdays and Christmas with me

Do not leave me out just because I cannot say yes. I want to be there

Read my body language – if I obviously want to be left alone – don't feel guilty about it
We all need our own space

Help me to keep my dignity as long as possible and don't be embarrassed – I am what I am

Never doubt that you didn't do your best for me

I appreciate everything you do for me – from the tiniest to the biggest gesture

Let me go when I'm ready

My photos and precious memorabilia will remind you of special times and bring a smile to your face on those sad and lonely days

Don't feel frightened by what is happening – my strength is deeper than you can see

Move on with your life because I have moved on to my next stage

Hang colourful decorative mobiles in my bedroom or in the lounge to help me to focus and engage, a shimmering or twinkling light can be exciting for me to watch

Provide an end of life tree in my care home where cherished memories can be left

Sit with me and feel comfortable together

Lay soft fabrics and silks over my chair or the bed or wrap around my shoulders or knees

Place orchids in my room, they last for a long time and require minimal attention, the colours are vibrant and engaging

Refer to my own personal life storybook or scrapbook, as this will trigger my memory and this will help us to communicate. Use key words, in the back of the book, props and familiar pictures and stories to give my life meaning

I would love to have artificial blossom trees or twinkling trees in the corner of my room

Record stories read by family members - a familiar voice that I recognise will provide relaxation and make me feel loved and wanted. It will also provide feelings of security and confidence

Learn basic hand massage with essential oils like lavender. Train family members - touch is the last sensation to go

Tap into my five senses...

Taste   I would love to have an ice lolly or cornet and a bowl of ice cold sorbet

Touch   I would enjoy a hand massage with essential oils or a soft hand cream

Give me a rummage box with scraps of different materials or ribbons

I love to fiddle with things that are within easy reach next to my chair or bed

Smell   Choose different aromas within the environment to stimulate my senses or my appetite - the smell of freshly baked cakes or bread or beautiful freshly cut flowers or a small bunch of herbs

Sound   Play soft relaxation music, birdsong, or gentle harp music, set a poetry CD running

Sight   Hang mobiles in the corner of the room or in the window where they catch the sunlight

Perhaps we can both enjoy these sensory activities together or they can help to stimulate me and keep me occupied when there is no one else around.

Play music of the appropriate era, 1920's - 1970's or maybe something more up-to date. I do not only need songs from my childhood. Remember the kind of music I enjoy. I may be more responsive to music from a time when I was 30 or 40 years old

Avoid sensory overload, a radio can often be over stimulating and annoying and frustrating if it just drones on in the background - close doors and windows, turn down the TV, consider moving me to a quieter environment if I am obviously looking uncomfortable or distressed

Provide visual stimulation with a fish tank, lava/glitter lamps - the soothing slow motion of moving liquid is relaxing and engaging

Speak gently to me because although I may not be able to understand the words the tone may be comforting

By knowing my life history you will find creative ways to connect and communicate with me

Use soft materials or soft toys to gently touch my cheek or neck

Avoid activities which involve fine motor skills as they can often be too fiddly or frustrating

Allow me to walk away from an activity if I choose to, I may well return to it in my own time so be patient and don't clear away the activity before I have given up on it

Offer me sensory stimulation in a quiet environment

Try swaying, rocking or marching for stimulating exercise

Bring me a cup of tea when you visit me, it can feel welcoming and form a bond and display of friendship

Just be there for me, it will help me to feel needed

Treat me with dignity and respect before and after death

Involve me and my family carers at an early stage when planning end of life care

Start with a simple opening sentence - "I really like your necklace" or "Your hair looks nice today", or make an observation of something in the room

Nature sounds can bring calm to my environment

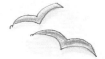

Be aware of any rituals I may have or any plans for dying

Help me to make preparations in order to sort out my personal affairs however small or insignificant they may seem to you. It's the little things that count

Avoid me feeling lonely or abandoned. Sing me a lullaby, a favourite hymn or song. It will help to provide a link with my childhood and the motherly love I felt

Offer me sips of water or moisten my mouth when I can no longer take fluids, this will alleviate my pain and distress in the last stages

Consider my spiritual, emotional and cultural needs

Collect trinkets from charity shops and second hand junk shops, they can trigger my personal and individual memories

Give me a handbag full of objects, a purse with some old coins, cotton handkerchiefs, an address book, a hairbrush and some lipstick or make up

Bring in a bunch of herbs, e.g. some lavender, so we can smell or talk about the colour, textures, gardens and perfumes - smell can often trigger memories and stories

Share your own personal photos or interesting objects with me. It doesn't all need to be about me. Other people's stories and interests are just as interesting and fun to learn about

Share personal family tales, stories and anecdotes

Do not be frightened of silence

Step out of your comfort zone, sing, dance, or act the fool with me

If I start making repetitive sounds try repeating the same sound I am expressing however strange or alien it may seem

If I make repetitive actions try toys with repetitive action like spinning tops or tap a drum

Allow me to hear the clear sound from the Tibetan singing bowl

Talk to me about local issues and gossip relating to familiar places

Share your own now and then stories with me

Bring in babies and young children, they will allow feelings of love, calm and security

Share your iPad, laptop, iPod or mobile phone with me - I may find it a fascinating and exciting process

Share quiet times together. You may initially feel awkward but a sense of peace, comfort and trust can often follow

Bring in your knitting, sewing or embroidery or even sit quietly and read to yourself. Your presence alone gives comfort and a sense of togetherness and the feeling of not being left alone

Companionship is often all that is needed

Organise and arrange items and objects around me

Respect my wishes and beliefs

If I become angry or physically aggressive try batting bubbles together in the air with a wooden spoon, it will remove tension and we may both end up laughing

Hold my hand, stroke my face, fiddle with or brush my hair

Think of my body like a chrysalis, the butterfly has now flown and if this is what you believe butterflies will be around you in your everyday activities

Open the window and let out my spirit

Cherish every moment and opportunity to be together, it is these moments you will remember and that will stay with you when I am no longer in the present

Create a sense of love, tenderness and calmness and allow me time to be in my own reality. I may well believe I have to collect my children from school or that my mother is coming to visit me - go along with my reality and do not lie to me but support the feelings and emotions I am expressing

An activity with me is much more than just doing - it is being there either in silence or in full active participation

Your grief will be as strong even though in your eyes I may have died long ago

Never give up hope, a smile will cheer us both on those dreary damp days that can make you feel low and full of despair so turn your frown upside-down and smile

If I choose to cuddle a teddy or doll don't be embarrassed - share the tender moments with me as it will provide me with comfort and company

Provide activities that relate to a job I once did. Give me materials or objects that are familiar to me e.g. dusters, a typewriter, stapler or pad of paper and pen, files, or tools, ladles and whisks, shorthand notebook, books or baskets. These familiar objects may trigger memories of work or home life and happy times when I felt needed and important as a mother, boss, or employee

String objects together. For example, choose from a box of bottle tops, pom poms, pot pourri bags, streamers, photo themed collages or paper flowers and use them for tactile exploration

Set up gentle sensory stimuli in my room, use bubble lights, fibre optic lights, light projection, and a variety of aromas - addressing all the senses

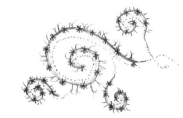

Take single words that I am expressing and string them together to make poems or sentences or just use as key words to trigger my memories

Provide me with sheets of paper or notebooks for scribbling notes or give me lists to copy. White window markers, the ones used in shop windows, can be fun. I can write my name or a poem on the glass in my room

Give me different types of art materials for painting and drawing such as pencils, charcoal, chalk and paint. You may need to make the first shape to start the drawing

Colour in either pictures from the Internet or circular drawings filled with symmetrical designs, or create pictures for me to colour in. Find an old spirograph set and make circular patterns to either cut out or colour in

Draw a square or round table and together we can fill in who sat around the table for mealtimes or special occasions. It will remind me of my family and my role as a parent or a child

Tear different colours from magazines or tissue paper or wallpaper samples and together we can stick on a pre-drawn picture e.g. a sunflower or garden, sea or sky scene – together we can make a beautiful sunset or rolling countryside from strips of paper or just an abstract colour collage

Provide me with a silk pillowcase to keep my skin wrinkle free

Change the fresh flowers in my bedroom regularly. Please never leave dead rotting flowers, they will upset the Feng Shui in my room

I may not want to take an active part in activities, just let me observe and make comments or just be there with no obvious intervention. However interactive I am, or not, that is fine

Play, explore, participate, engage with me. Let us discover things together, make it mutually meaningful, give and receive, all can be very fulfilling and enrich both of us

Activities based on gestures

Inspiration taken from the book 'Chocolate Rain'
by Sarah Zoutewelle

Use activities based on gestures:-

Tapping/Patting - use clay or bread dough or tap out rhythms using sticks, spoons or instruments

Stroking & Cuddling - petting animals or toys, ironing or drying of dishes

Pressing & Picking - stickers or gluing down, sand to make shapes, bubble wrap or poppers on clothes, activity cushions, peeling fruit e.g. satsumas

Pulling & Wrapping - dressing or undressing dolls or packages, pulling at knotted cord, 'row ,row ,row' the boat action songs, wrapping a present or a bandage

Open Palm - drawing on hand with non - toxic paints or water soluble marker, games hiding objects in hands or covered with a tea towel

Grabbing and Grasping - throwing soft balls or wool, scrunch paper, grasping objects, hand games

Pairing - gloves, socks, slippers

Folding - papers or newspapers, bed clothes, laundry or tea towels

Rubbing - polishing brass, washing clothes, polishing tables, windows or mirrors, iPad games

Rolling - balls on table, pastry, rain tubes, paint rollers

Winding - fishing reels, wool balls, wool or ribbon around tubes

Tearing - strips of paper for papier mâché, strips of cloth, tearing magazines and tissue paper for collages

Waving and Swaying - silks and feathers, ribbons, scarves

Stacking - toys and plant pots

Rummaging - fleecy blankets

Threading & Sliding - laces and wooden puzzles

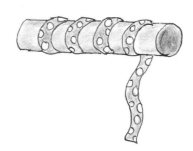

Strum a guitar or play a musical instrument so I can sing along or play a tune. This could be in either the bedroom or together in the communal areas

Use dolls, mascots, soft toy animals, comfort blankets to provide a sense of comfort and security, the holding of objects can be really comforting in their own right

Be my companion and create a special one to one connection with me

Read me 'Wind in the Willows', an interactive story from my iPad. Allow me to turn the pages and touch the screen

Tell me what day or date it is even if I don't respond

Be my strength, my guide and my lifeline. Never give up on me

The space around me is important, leave things where I can reach them

Read me a recipe or two. Give me a pile of recipe books to look through

Bring in a kaleidoscope and show me the bright colours

Reduce stress and anxiety by giving me a gentle hand massage, it provides comfort and a deep connection and enhances relaxation

Keep all my skin moisturised daily not just my hands and face

Never stop bringing me flowers or decorating my room

Put on my lipstick (lippy) or help me to do it myself

Play with iFish or the sand Garden on my iPad

Leave bells or buzzers close by so I can contact you

Don't forget about my feet. I want more than just the chiropodist. Sometimes arrange for someone to massage or cream them or better still a pedicure or reflexology session - touch is a very important sense

Give me fresh sheets and pyjamas/nightdresses regularly

Give me a selection of melon, fresh fruit salad, ice lollies or chocolate

Fiddle with my hair and let me fiddle with yours

Cleanse and moisturise my face everyday

Laugh and cry together

Use props, hats, facial expressions and take risks

Always be flexible, improvise and adapt whenever carrying out activities with me

Be creative with your storytelling and drama, sing me a nursery rhyme and read me a classic children's story

Give me warm bubbly water for my hands and feet, sometimes with ducks or other floating objects

Place a warm lavender wheat bag around my neck or in my bed, it is warm and comforting

Write down any of my special memories or my snippets of conversation, it can be comforting for my relatives to read

Keep the air fresh and open the window

Use objects that are special and mean something to me e.g. "the most beautifullest Mum in the world" mug or the "I love you" mug

Touch my hand or hair in that special way that means something to both of us

Keep close to hand my treasure box with my most sentimental and personal items: my cross, my Buddha, my angels, my worry dolls, my sheepskin, my rings, my jewellery and my soft toys or teddies

Have lots of pillows available so I can always sit up if I want to when my visitors call

Keep me as mobile as possible, for as long as possible.
Allow me to sit unsupported with supervision on a daily basis

Try to avoid asking me direct, specific questions that require a factual response - enjoy the memories rather than making me feel I am being tested

Take me through some simple Chinese martial arts - tai chi or qigong exercises - together we can do some simple physical movements, meditation or breathing exercises. These will positively affect my mind, body and spirit and can be easily achieved passively with the help from my friends, family or carer or actively copying movements

Don't expect too much from me, be realistic. You may need to be more flexible and adaptable

Make sure I do some form of active or passive exercise everyday

Don't feel guilty about allowing others in to help me. Sometimes a new face can be a refreshing change for all concerned

Place a bird feeder outside my window

Allow me to rock back and forwards or call out the same words or sounds if I choose to. Don't worry about me if I seem calm when doing this, it may be my way of coping with the confused world around me. But please intervene if I become distressed, I may be in pain, constipated, hungry or dehydrated

I may see, hear or smell things that are not really there i.e. hallucinate, depending on my type of dementia or I may become delusional and have a distorted view of what is happening around me. Please comfort me and distract me from my fears. Linking into my key words or topics that you know make me feel good and comforted

I may feel restless and want to walk around. Provide me with some physical activity to enable me to feel calm. I would love to rock in a rocking chair

If I have a hearing aid please ensure the batteries are working and it is clean and functioning properly

Check regularly if I am too hot, too cold, hungry, thirsty, or if I need the toilet – I may not be able to tell you myself

Keep me on the move or turn me regularly, I don't want to get pressure sores, my heels and elbows are just as much at risk as my bottom

Keep me mobile and improve my circulation, this will prevent infections and possible blood clots

I may become severely confused – known as delirium, often caused by infections. If you notice any changes in my behaviour or increased confusion please contact my GP or nurse immediately

Clean my teeth or dentures regularly and ensure I have regular dental appointments. Check my dentures fit correctly so I can still speak and eat well

If you notice that I am not eating check my gums are not sore or ulcerated

If my mobility reduces suddenly – check my feet or that my shoes are still comfortable. Are my slippers worn and not easy to keep on?

If I want to make a living will, as it used to be known, or an advance directive (an advance decision to refuse treatment - ADRT), this needs to be done early on in my dementia so I can make decisions on the treatments at end of life

I may also want to make a lasting power of attorney so someone can make decisions for me about my treatment once I am unable to do this for myself

Sometimes just cuddle me and hold me close

Always ensure my glasses are clean and my prescription is current. Keep my glasses with me at all times.

Make sure I have a tissue or handkerchief nearby or tucked in a pocket or my sleeve

Allow my grandchildren to play in my room, their laughter will bring me joy and a smile to my face - I do not need to be in silence.

Allow me to soak in the bath – make it a pleasurable experience, not just a practical task. Wrap me in big soft fluffy towels large enough to cover me totally and don't rush the drying – I may want to sit or lie around with my towel afterwards

Keep my hair washed and looking good

And finally be there at the end as a closure for you, as well as to experience peace

Talk to me right to the end

The end is not the end - spend time with me afterwards and together we will be at peace. It is a lasting special moment that never leaves you

Hold my hand and when I'm gone stay with me for a while, lay down next to me, be at peace with me

Let me go and... please don't forget about me.

So what do we need to make it as good as it can be?

Time   **Patience**   **Silence**

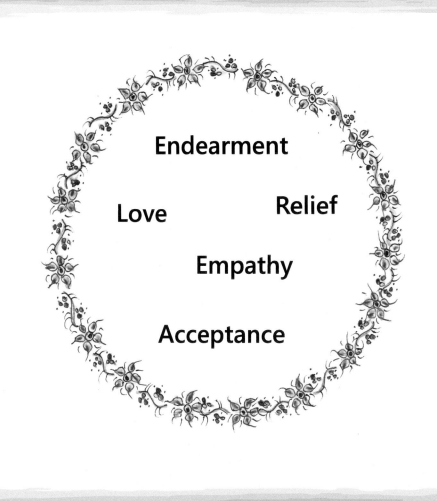

Consideration

Peace   Pleasure

Tranquility

Risk

Other things that I would like to happen...

My special wish...

One thing about me I want people to remember...

Like the snow that melts on a bright spring day,
you will slowly and gently watch me slip away

But please don't be sad or stricken by grief,
just think of me now as a golden autumn leaf

It changes its colour and floats to the ground...

...but in spring again it seems to appear with no sound

Its vibrant soft bud pushes out from the tree,
and offers delight to all who can see

It brightens the day and gives off a bright light
and will lift up your heart and help with your fight

So watch me return to you each and every spring,
a skip to your step and some joy I will bring

So you'll never forget me when
spring's on its way...

...as the flowers they will blossom
and brighten your day